Teach English Abroad: Some Guy's Quick and Straightforward How-To Guide for Teaching English Overseas Along with Tips and Tricks to Be Successful at It

By Jeremy Rasmussen

Check out my homepage at:
www.LearnJapaneseFromSomeGuy.com

My Japanese grammar textbook:
www.amazon.com/dp/B013D2FDMG

My YouTube channel:
youtube.com/c/learnjapanesefromsomeguy

Table of Contents

Chapter 1: A Quick Introduction

"Adventure is worthwhile." – Aesop

I suppose, as manners would dictate, before we get started I should introduce myself. Hello, 初めまして, mucho gusto, and 你好. My name is Jeremy, and I am just *some guy* who has spent the last seven years of his life traveling the world; seeing the sights, learning languages, trying interesting foods, meeting amazing people, and having unforgettable experiences... all while getting paid!(mostly) As a matter of fact, I am writing this book from my apartment in China. But what is this amazing job that allows one to do all of these wonderful things, you ask? I suspect you already know the answer, but I will tell you anyway... teaching English, of course!

After graduating from college and still not knowing exactly what I wanted to do with my life, I decided to try and tick one of the items off of my bucket list, which was to visit Japan. But then I got to thinking... why just *visit* Japan? That's a big investment of time and money (especially for a newly-graduated young adult like myself with a mountain of student loans to pay off), just to spend a week or two (at *most*) over there. That wouldn't be worth it. I couldn't possibly get the whole "Japanese experience," especially when two days would be wasted on travel time alone! Not to mention the jet-lag… "I know!" I thought to myself, "Why don't I *live* in Japan? But how? Even though I just graduated from college, I have no real skills, and I don't know anybody over there. What could I possibly offer anyone that would allow me to call Japan my home?" Then it hit me like a sack of raw fish… I could teach English! And that's basically how I got started on my world traveling adventure, and I haven't looked back since.

I lived and worked in Japan for about four and a half years, seven months in Spain, and currently reside in China, where I teach at a local high school. I haven't decided where I want to go next, but I have never been to South America, and Brazil has always seemed like a pretty cool place… Can you say, "Carnival?"

Anyway, the reason I am writing this book is not just brag about my life (well… maybe a little), but to help inform and educate those who would like to do the same (travel the world that is, not brag about their lives). This book will certainly not answer *every* question you may have, nor give every necessary piece of advice you may need, but I will do my best to impart onto you the wisdom I have picked up over the years, and how I think you *too* can make your experience abroad as memorable and meaningful as possible.## Chapter 2: Just Do it Already, Would Ya?

"The man who goes alone can start today; but he who travels with another must wait till that other is ready."

— Henry David Thoreau

One of the most common things people say when they find out what I do for a living is, "I wish *I* could do that!" And my response to them is always, "You can!!!" (I always make sure to yell it, to help drive the point home. Thus, the three exclamation marks.) People have this idea that you have to be some special individual, or have some amazing skill to go teach in a foreign country. Let me be the first to tell you, in case you didn't already know, that is absolutely *not* the case. I will go into further detail later regarding the requirements one must meet before setting off on their journey in Chapter 11, but let me just say now, if you speak English natively, you are already qualified to work abroad *some*where.

Another question I often get is "How do you do it?" Of course, they're not asking about the processes and procedures one must typically go through to find a position abroad (I will talk about that in Chapter 4), but rather how I found the resolve, the internal fortitude, the *chutzpah* to make the decision and actually go through with it. And I always think, "You mean, how do I make the decision to fly around the world to a country I've always wanted to go to, live among the people, make great new friends, learn another language, learn about a whole new culture, and see and experience things that would otherwise be impossible?" My question to anyone who would ask "How do you do it?" would be "Who wouldn't do it?"

The fact that you're reading this book (thanks, by the way) is indicative in and of itself that you are at least somewhat interested in teaching abroad. My best advice to you, if you're still not sure whether you can "actually do it," is to just stop over-thinking it.

Depending on where you go and what kind of contract you sign, at most, you'll likely only be away from home for a year. And that's if you decide you don't want to break your contract. If you go abroad and decide it's not for you (which of course happens), there's nothing to stop you from breaking your contract and heading home early. But the point is, it's not like once you make the decision to go somewhere you're *stuck* there. You can go home whenever you want. But don't focus on the negative! The potential positive outcomes *far* outweigh the potential negative outcomes.

I originally only planned to stay in Japan for two years, but I enjoyed it so much and had such a great time that before I knew it, it nearly became five! Anyway, my main point here is that if you're thinking about doing it, just do it. Stop saying that you're going to do it, or that you *want* to do it. Just do it already! Don't let yourself or someone else talk you out of it. Trust me. You'll be glad you did.

Chapter 3: What Are the Benefits of Teaching Abroad

"The gladdest moment in human life, me thinks, is a departure into unknown lands." – Sir Richard Burton

If you're still not convinced that teaching abroad is for you, let me try to persuade you by telling you about all of the amazing benefits that come from living and working in a foreign country, as if they weren't obvious enough without me having to explain them.

By *far* the most beneficial consequence (sure, consequences can be positive) of teaching abroad, in my humble opinion, is the acquisition of another language. Talk about a way to open doors! Imagine how many potential employers will be beating down your door (perhaps even that one you just opened) when they see that not only do you have experience living and working abroad, but that you speak German, French, Russian, or Korean, too. In today's day and age, where a college degree means almost nothing, you absolutely need another way to stand out among the crowd. Bi or even tri-linguality (it's a word…) is definitely one of the best ways to do it.

Unfortunately, a lot of people (*too many* people, in my opinion) go abroad and don't take advantage of the amazing opportunity to learn a second language. I will go into more detail later on why I think this is "bad," but just know that learning another language will help you out in a number of ways, and that you should really prepare yourself put some effort into it.

Another obvious benefit of teaching abroad is that you get to see the world. I've found that that's the one dream that everyone always seems to share, "Oh, I want to see the world. I want to travel. I want to go places and do things!" they say. Numerous studies and surveys have shown that one of the biggest regrets the elderly have when they look back on their lives is not having traveled and seen the world. It only gets harder as you get older, so why not take advantage of the opportunity now, before it's too late? Though I'd be lying if I said to you that schools don't have a preference when it comes to the ages of their teachers (more on this in Chapter 6), but the reality is that they will accept people of (almost) all ages. One of my co-workers, Gabby, is in his late forties. And another teacher I worked with here in China was in his mid to late fifties and, despite the fact that he was a *colossal* jerk, they still hired him. So, don't think that just because you're "old" (or even a jerk) that you can't do it. You can!

Another great benefit of living and working abroad is having the opportunity to learn about and immerse yourself in a whole new culture. Going to school is a good way to get an education, but if you want to *really* learn something, then you absolutely *must* travel. As cliché as it sounds, you will grow tremendously as a person and learn things that cannot possibly be taught in a textbook. I know that personally my experiences abroad have opened my mind and eyes to things that would have otherwise remained hidden and unseen. You are sure to experience the same thing if you give yourself the opportunity.

Meeting new people is another great reason to teach abroad. I cannot tell you how many amazing people I have met throughout my travels. People often ask me if I miss my friends and family while I am away. Of course I do. But when I am back home, I miss the friends and family I have made overseas. If you are an outgoing, social person (which is kind of a prerequisite for ESL teachers), then you will no doubt make many new life-long friends during your adventures as well.

I touched on this earlier, but, especially for younger people, being able to write on your résumé that you have actual experience living and working abroad will be *huge* in your future career, almost no matter what that career may be. The advantages teaching abroad will give you over competition for the same job will no doubt help put you over the top.

Chapter 4: How Do I Find a Job Abroad?

"Broad, wholesome, charitable views of men and things cannot be acquired by vegetating in one little corner of the earth all of one's lifetime." – Mark Twain

Now that I have convinced you that teaching English abroad is a worthwhile venture, your next question is probably, "How do I go about actually *finding* a teaching position?"

Well, that's a great question, and you're very smart for asking it, but, unfortunately, it's a little difficult to answer. Well, it's actually quite simple to answer. I should say that it's difficult to answer *satisfactorily*, but I will try my best.

The first thing you must do is decide *where* you want to teach (see chapter 10 for a list of common teaching destinations). Different organizations will help you find jobs in different countries. Some organizations may deal with Asian countries, while another organization will deal with European countries, and, as you can imagine, not every school is the same in regards to what it requires from potential teachers.

I will tell you what I did to find my jobs in Japan, Spain, and China, and then give other sources that will surely help you in your quest to get to where *you* want to go.

First, let's talk Japan.

When I first decided that I wanted to teach in Japan, I simply googled "Teach English in Japan." I clicked on the first link, which was from a company called AEON. After reading all of the information on their page, I felt that AEON would be a good company to work for. But before actually applying, I did another Google search on AEON, something to the effect of "What is it like to work at AEON?" I then read different articles (mostly blogs) about people's experiences. After reading mostly positive things, I decided that I would indeed like to work for them and applied (I recommend doing this same kind of "research" for the company/organization for which you wish to work). If Japan is where you think you'd like to go, you can apply and find out more information about AEON here: www.aeonet.com.

Another option, if you're looking to go to Japan, is with the JET program. I had actually considered trying to get a job through JET while I waited to hear back from AEON about my application, only to find that I had missed the deadline to apply. They only accept applications at the end of the year. So, if you don't apply during the winter of 2016, for instance, you'll have to wait until winter of 2017 to apply for the *2018* school year! Time-wise, it's a pretty difficult program to deal with, so you have to plan ahead.

After starting the application process with JET, it takes about four months to hear whether or not you were accepted. Information about JET, along with its application time line can be found here: www.jetprogramusa.org.

Another option to work in Japan, if AEON and the JET program don't work out for you, is to be an ALT (Assistant Language Teacher). Whereas the JET program is sponsored by the government, ALT's are typically hired by a recruiter or directly by the school that needs a teacher.

Links to useful websites and sources for finding work in Japan (and other countries) can be found at the end of this book in chapter 17.

After leaving Japan, my next teaching destination was Spain.

Just like when I was looking for work in Japan, I simply googled "Teach English in Spain" to find my next employment opportunity.

Like I have said already, there are hundreds of different organizations and ways to go abroad, but I ended up finding my way to Spain through an organization called CIEE, which can be found (not surprisingly) at www.CIEE.org.

They offer a number of positions in, as of this time of this writing, 11 different countries; Chile, China, the Czech Republic, Dominican Republic, Morocco, Peru, Senegal, South Korea, Spain, Thailand, and Vietnam.

Through CIEE, I went to Spain on a volunteer program where I worked at a local high school two or three hours a day as an assistant teacher in basically all of the subjects. Since I wasn't being paid any money, a host-family was found for me to live with during my stay there.

It was my first time living with a host family and I absolutely loved it. I built some amazing relationships, and we still communicate regularly. In fact, my "little brother" just started college! Oh, he's so grown up now. Where does the time go...

But if money isn't your goal for teaching, I definitely recommend going the volunteer route. You'll have a great time and volunteer experience is always good to be able to write on a résumé. Of course, there are many paid positions available through CIEE as well. Look through them and find the one that works best for you.

Finally, let's talk about China.

To get my job here in China where I currently reside, I was actually just kind of, well... lucky.

My brother is friends with a guy named Alex whose mother's job is to actually find and place English teachers in various schools around China. I told Alex I was interested in going to China and he gave me his mother's contact information. She and I exchanged a few e-mails, and before I knew it, she had found me this absolutely amazing position as a teacher at a high school.

Naturally, not everyone knows a Chinese guy named Alex whose mother can find them a job teaching English, but I think it's important for you to realize that someone you know (or perhaps a friend of a friend) can most likely put you in *direct* contact with someone like

Alex who *can*. You'd be surprised by how many people you know or talk to every day that went abroad themselves to teach, or know someone that did.

As a matter of fact, my two newest co-workers found their jobs here the same way. No, not through Alex... They had a friend who put them in touch with a friend, and now they're here.

Is there another way to go abroad and not be a teacher?

Teaching isn't for everyone, but if you still feel like you want to live abroad for a while and see a different part of the world, you still have a couple of options.

One option is being an au pair. "What is an 'au pair,'" you ask? I actually didn't know until quite recently either, but an au pair is *like* an English teacher, except instead of working at a school, you live with a family and informally teach the *family* English. In exchange, they will let you live with them and provide you with food and a place to sleep.

When I was living in Spain, a Spanish friend of mine wanted to have someone come live with them and teach their three year old son English. I made a post about it on Facebook, and one of my friends said she was interested. A couple of months later she was living in Spain having a grand ol' time.

What the family will provide you with and require of you obviously varies from family to family. Some might ask you to "work" 20 hours a week, or three hours a night from 5:00 to 8:00, or whatever. It all depends on their schedule. Some families might even give you some spending money.

Some people, like my friend, have wonderful experiences and make life-long friendships. Others, unfortunately, have bad experiences they wish they could forget. So, if you do decide to go the au pair route, be sure you know what you're getting into before making the commitment. Some things you may want to consider are:

- How many hours a week will you be required to "be at home?"

- How much freedom will you have? Will there be a curfew? Will the family give you your own key?

- How many children does the family have (if any)?

- Other than teaching English, what other expectations are there (cooking, cleaning, etc.)

- Will you have your own room?

- How long will you stay?

- Does anyone in the family speak English well (in case of emergencies)?

- Will the family provide you with an allowance, if so, how much?

- Would they be willing to drive you places?

- If you're a vegetarian, will they provide vegetarian meals?

One thing to remember is that as an au pair, you won't likely be able to stay at your new home for very long. It depends on where you want to go and what your home country's relationship is with your destination country.

If you're an American, for instance, you can go to most European countries *without* a visa for 90 days. If you want to stay longer, you'll need a visa (working or student). But if you're going as an au pair, you most likely won't be able to get a visa since you're not a student and you're technically not "working," at least in any capacity that your host country can tax you on.

If you're looking solely for the experience of going abroad and immersing yourself in a new culture (albeit for only a short while), the au pair route can be a great option. As you can probably imagine, most families look for female au pairs, but guys can do it, too.

I've never personally used this website, but it seems to be one of the most popular among people looking for work as an au pair: www.greataupair.com.

Getting your passport

If you already have your passport (good for you!) then you can skip this section and go down to the "Applying for Visas" section.

If you don't have a passport, however, then the first thing you absolutely *must* do (after reading this book and telling all of your friends about it, of course) is get one.

The passport application process is quite easy, albeit a little time consuming, but you definitely want to get this taken care of as soon as possible. It would be *terrible* if you couldn't take advantage of a dream employment opportunity simply because you had to wait "six to eight weeks" to get your passport in the mail, and you couldn't apply.

Every country has different procedures when it comes to applying for and obtaining a passport. I'd recommend just doing a quick Google search of something like "How to apply for a passport" to get information specific for your country.

Applying for visas

For those of you who don't know exactly what a visa is, I will explain quickly.

Having a passport alone is usually enough to let you travel to most countries and spend a limited amount of time there, but if you want to spend an extended period of time somewhere, then you also need a visa. There are many kinds of visas; working, tourist, student (all of which have their own different sub-categories) and your new employer will tell you what kind you need to apply for so that you can legally work in the country and stay longer than the typical tourist would be able to.

Usually, the school that is sponsoring your visa will simply have you apply for a sort of "temporary" visa that will let you legally work for a short period of time (usually a month, or so). Then before that visa expires, they will help you apply for a longer lasting one.

I've already mentioned that there can be a lot of effort involved when you want to find a job teaching abroad.

Sifting through the seemingly endless amount of information is enough to bog just about *anyone* down. In fact, I often times thought of giving up myself after spending hours googling and researching, only to find that I hadn't made any progress at all in finding out any useful or relevant information.

But even after you do all of your research, find a reputable school, fill out all of the required paper work, write the required essays (if there are any), do the interview(s), wait around for a couple of months, and *finally* get the job, you're still only about halfway done. Oh, the humanity!

Perhaps the most challenging part of the whole ordeal, in my opinion, is just *getting* your visa.

If you are fortunate enough to have a consulate of the country you are going to in your area, then this step will be a *lot* less stressful for you (though, you can bet it will still be stressful). If you're like most people, however, you'll probably have to do a bit of traveling to get all of the visa paperwork taken care of.

In Arizona (my home state), for example, there is no Chinese consulate. So, I had to actually make the seven hour drive to the consulate in L.A. in order to do all of the paperwork. And I certainly can't speak for all consulates when I say this, but they are typically just big, disorganized messes. Their websites give phone numbers that are either out-of-service, or don't get you in touch with the people you were looking for. The e-mail addresses given in the "contact us" section are either wrong, or the people to whom they belong just never feel like writing back. Regardless of what country you're hoping to go to, you will likely need to have a lot of patience and be able to deal with a lot of "not smart" people if you wish to eventually attain that coveted seal.

If you do have to go out of state to apply for a visa, though, one useful tip I can give is that even if a consulate tells you that they absolutely *cannot* send you back your passport through the mail, or will not allow anyone but *you* to pick it up in person, it's *probably* not true.

While it is true that the consulate itself cannot legally send you your passport with your (hopefully) freshly minted visa through the mail, the little office that is likely set up just *right* down the hall (that is not officially associated with the consulate), on the other hand, will be more than happy to do it for you… for a small fee, of course.

This was really helpful for me because it meant I could immediately go back home after submitting all of my paperwork, as opposed to having to hang around another day (or more) in an unfamiliar town with nowhere to go until my visa paperwork was fully processed. If you can get a hold of someone at the consulate office (Hah! Good luck!), be sure to ask them about the possibility of hiring a third-party to mail you back your passport.

And just to be on the safe side, I would bring *triple* copies of all of your required documentation to the consulate. It can be easy in the hustle and bustle of everything to misplace a paper or two, which could delay (or potentially *ruin*) any chance you had of successfully applying for your visa. And even if the consulate's website doesn't explicitly tell you they need something, if you think it could be a possibility bring it anyway (copy of birth certificate, social security card, bank account information with balances, criminal history report, etc.).

In order to get my Chinese visa, for example, I was informed (only upon my arrival at the consulate itself, of course) that I needed to also provide a copy of my driver's license. Fortunately, when I had applied for my Spanish visa, I also needed to give copies of my driver's license. Knowing that this might be a possibility when applying for my Chinese visa (even though it wasn't written anywhere as a requirement on their website), I made sure to bring a couple of copies of it, and I was glad that I did.

One last thing that is important to note about visas, however, is that once you have one, the company you're working for can't do anything to get it taken away. So, if you're working for a school and they sponsor you for a three-year visa and you quit (or get fired) after only a month into the job, you are still legally allowed to live and work in that country with another school for the remainder of those three years.

I've heard stories about companies/schools deceiving employees on this point. But just know that once you have that visa, it's good until it expires. Some people even lie to deceive schools into sponsoring their visas for a couple of years, only to quit soon afterward! But you wouldn't do that, would you?

Chapter 5: The Differences Between a Public School and a Privately Owned English Training Center

"Life is either a daring adventure or nothing."
– Helen Keller

As you sift through all of the information regarding positions for English teachers, you'll likely come across two distinct choices; working for a public school, or working for a privately owned English training center.

If you have spent most of your life in the U.S., you may not even be that familiar with language training centers. I know there weren't any around my area where I grew up. But all over the world, teaching English is *big* business. Many entrepreneurial types open up their own schools where people of all ages can come and take English courses. And that is essentially what an English training center is; a privately owned business, where the service they sell is the teaching of English.

That is easy enough to understand, right? But what are the differences between working at public school versus a training center? Since I have experience with both, I feel like I can answer some common questions about the two and give some insight to help you make your decision.

"Which provides a higher salary?"

The salaries of the two vary (sometimes quite dramatically), depending on the country you're in and the training center/school you're working for, so it is difficult to say which will net you more money. If you're going in with absolutely *no* experience, then I would imagine that you'll typically make more money at a training center. If, however, you have years of experience and a degree of some kind, your salary at a public school will naturally be higher, as most training centers typically don't take one's background into as much consideration as public schools do when determining teachers' salaries.

"Which do you prefer to work at?"

They both have their own positive and negative aspects, and I'm sure people have different feelings based on their own personal experiences, but, overall, I definitely enjoy working at a public school more than a training center.

"Why do you prefer working at a public school?"

It is much more accurate to call a training center a "business" than a "school." And it is much more accurate to call the people who come to your training center "customers" than "students." I've always disliked this aspect of training centers. As a teacher at a training center, you will sometimes be put in awkward situations where you have to exaggerate the truth (or just strait up lie) in order to keep a student from leaving. Imagine, for instance, that your student, Tomofumi, wants to quit your school because he feels his English isn't improving. There is absolutely *no* way your boss would allow you to simply agree with him and let him leave. Even if he is right and his English hasn't improved at all, you will have to say something like, "No, Tomofumi! Your English has gotten a *lot* better. And I'm sure if you sign up for our newest course, it will continue to improve." You may end up sometimes feeling more like a salesman than a teacher.

At the training center where I worked, for instance, there were a number of different classes based on the skill level of the students. Theoretically, after a student finishes Class A, he or she should be ready for Class B, and after they finish Class B, he or she should be ready for Class C, and so on. However, it's not so uncommon for a student who finishes Class B to *not* be ready for Class C. In cases like this, the school will initially try to get the student to take Class B again, but most students don't want to pay money to take the exact same course. Naturally, they want to "move up." So, sometimes the student will be put in a class that will almost definitely be too difficult for them. This student will then basically ruin the class and make your job *much* harder. And what do you think will happen after this student finishes Class C and wants to move on to Class D? Unless the student is especially motivated, it's a vicious kind of cycle that is nearly impossible to break.

"What things do you like about working at a training center?"

Variety - Training centers definitely offer much more of a variety when it comes to the classes you will teach and to whom you will teach them. When I was working in Japan, for instance, I would teach a group of seven to eight year old children their ABC's, and then after that class immediately go and teach a group of college students advanced level English. This variety can definitely keep the job "exciting" or, at the very least, more "fresh," as many of your classroom experiences will be different from one lesson to the next.

Class size - Class sizes are also much smaller at training centers. The average number of students in my classes was about five. Sometimes I would only have one or two, though, and at most I would have ten. (just as a side-note, my favorite number of students in a class was four)

If you have never taught before, you would be surprised by just how much more challenging it is to teach a large group than a small one. And since most public school classes can have up to 30 students (or more!), the challenge of teaching and maintaining order in a public school classroom just grows exponentially. That's one reason why I think it is better to get experience working at a training center before working at a public school.

Student-teacher relationships - Another nice thing is that since most students who will come to your training center are adults, you can build more "real" relationships. This was perhaps one of my favorite things about working in Japan; getting to know my students on a personal level. As you work, many students will come and go, but sometimes you will have a student who sticks around for a long time. I had students in Japan that were studying at the training center before I arrived, and were *still* there when I left (four years later). Naturally, we became close and I consider some of them actual friends. In fact, I still keep in touch with a few of them. I can't really see something like this happening at a public school.

The atmosphere - The atmosphere at a training center is typically much more fun and lighthearted. As you can imagine, students at public schools are usually not very happy to be there, which doesn't make for the most positive learning environment in the world (especially Chinese students, with their 14 hour school days. Yes,

14 hours!). As I mentioned before, training centers are just businesses, so students having a *good time* is actually *more* important than them learning anything, as odd as that sounds. Teachers are encouraged to make jokes and keep the class "fun." At AEON, I used to love sitting in the lobby before class joking around with all of my students. Many times, classes at public schools feel like slave-driving, which can really start to wear you down mentally after a while. Just take a look at my Chinese students' desks and tell me you wouldn't get bummed out looking at this every day.

No homework - I imagine most training centers don't give their students homework, at least not in the traditional sense. Naturally, students may be given extra material to study or do at home on their own, but for the most part, a majority of the learning takes place in the classroom. This is great for teachers because that means they won't have any homework to take home themselves and grade or correct. You can imagine how time consuming it can be for a public school teacher to read and grade 60 or more ten page essays.

One of the best things about working at a training center is that you almost never bring work home, and once you leave the office, you are essentially "free." Public school teachers, on the other hand, may have to meet with parents, deal with students working on assignments, grade papers, and so on, on their days off.

"What do you like about working at a public school?"

The workload - From my own personal experience, I can say that the workload at a training center *far* outweighs that of a public school. When I was working in Japan (at an English training center), I would teach, on average, five classes a day (50 minutes each) during the week and seven or eight on Saturdays. Five classes in one day isn't *so* bad, but teaching eight in one day is an absolute *killer*. I was basically standing *all* day, and after years of doing that, I seriously started having back problems. Teaching definitely ain't for sissies...

This is in *stark* contrast to my current job at a public school where I teach just 12 classes a week (40 minutes a class). Yes, you read that right; 12 classes in an *entire* week. It's crazy when I think about it. I mean, I almost worked that much in a single *day* in Japan (while making less money!). I know that after having worked here and gotten used to this style of teaching, it would be hard for me to go back to a non-public school.

Naturally, not everyone can expect to land as cushy a job as mine, but, for the most part, teaching at a public is a bit "easier."

The salary - If you have a degree and a number of years of experience, teaching at a public school will generally earn you more money than you would otherwise make at a training center.

Vacation days - The amount of vacation you get working for a public school is *insane* by almost any standard. School teachers often complain that they don't get paid enough, but when you take into consideration how much time they spend *not* working, I would say the pay is *absolutely* commensurate.

Having Saturdays and Sundays off is almost a given for any public school. Though, in some Asian countries, you may have to work a Saturday or Sunday every once in a while. But seeing as how they are government institutions, they also get every national holiday off. Then, of course, there are the "special event days." As I write this, my school's annual "sports meeting," which lasts two days, is being held. So, instead of going to class, students are having what we in the U.S. would likely call "field-day." What am I doing during this time then, you ask? Aside from writing this book... NOTHING. My classes for today and tomorrow are canceled and so I now get two unexpected days off in the middle of my work-week. Can't beat that! There are also a number of days where students take trips, have testing, etc., where classes for the day are canceled, as well. They're always such nice little surprises, like a snow-day!

The greatest of all, however, is of course summer vacation. Can you think of another job where employees get *two* months of *paid* vacation every year? It's crazy. If you decide to work for a public school, be sure to find out about their summer vacation policy; Does your salary get reduced during that time? Will they pay for a plane ticket back home? Will you be required to teach summer classes?

Naturally, training centers don't have any of these "special event days," and they certainly don't have summer vacations. In fact, on many days where public schools close, you will still have to work, since that just means more students will be available to come and take *your* classes.

Chapter 6: Is the Industry Racist?

"Investment in travel is an investment in yourself." – Matthew Karsten

People sometimes ask me, "Is the industry racist?" And my answer is that it's not *racist* so much as it is *discriminatory* (I will try to explain what I mean further down). That isn't to say, of course, that the *people* or *students* discriminate against teachers. I would say, and regrettably so, that it is the *industry* itself that has the issue.

I remember when after having finished my interview to work in Japan, I told my friend Lars (who had also taught in Japan years before as an English teacher) that I wasn't exactly confident in getting the job. He looked at me and said, "Oh, c'mon, Jeremy. You are young, tall, have blonde hair and blue eyes, some might even say semi-attractive, and, above all, you are white. You are exactly what they are looking for! I'm almost positive they will hire you." And of course, he was right. They did hire me. But I like to think it was based more on the potential they saw in me, and not so much on my skin tone or dreamy baby-blue eyes.

That isn't to say that schools abroad absolutely *won't* hire people of non-Anglo-Saxon heritage, of course. My former co-worker here in China, Gabby, was straight up *from* Africa. And while working in Japan, I had one co-worker whose parents were both Chinese (she grew up in Canada), and another whose parents were both Thai (he grew up in Scotland, of all places) So, it isn't difficult at all for non-whites to find work teaching abroad, but it would be a lie to say that Caucasians don't have an advantage.

And I understand that despite having begun this chapter by saying that "the industry is not racist," some of what I said sounds an awful lot like racism. But I will explain.

I prefer to use the word "discriminatory" because *everyone* is discriminated against. Schools generally prefer that their foreign teachers be young and attractive (*especially* training centers). We can imagine a situation where there are two potential teachers a school could hire; one is 30 years old and the other 45. All else being equal, the school would almost certainly hire the 30 year old. If the teachers were the exact same age and had the exact same credentials, they would then base their decision on which teacher was more attractive (which is why you sometimes may have to include a picture of yourself in your application to some places). This idea is appalling to most people in the West, but that's how other countries without sexual discrimination laws (particularly in Asia) operate.

In fact, I have found that people in Asia place a *lot* more emphasis and importance on one's physical appearance than we seem to do in the West (if you can imagine). Being "handsome" or "pretty" is paramount to almost anything else. If the 30 year old teacher from above were black and attractive and the 45 year old teacher were white and average looking, I'm sure a vast majority of schools would hire the attractive, black 30 year old.

But this should really come as a particular surprise to anyone because I think this kind of mentality can be applied to almost *any* industry (I mean, would you rather see an underwear model working the counter at Starbucks, or Mr. Rogers?) The reason I think it's worth mentioning here is because these qualities (age, attractiveness, how "foreign-looking" one is) play a much larger role than they typically would in other fields.

The reason is because, in addition to simply teaching the students English, you also act as an advertisement for your school. Your picture, for example, will likely be placed on the school's website. A picture of a young, attractive teacher will be much more effective at recruiting students than a picture of an older, less attractive teacher would. And you better believe the school will want to "show you off" and show the parents and students how great the school is because they can afford to hire a foreign teacher.

In fact, I would venture to say that if we took the same two teachers from before; an attractive 30 year old with no teaching experience and a frumpy 45 year old with years of experience, many schools would still be willing to hire the 30 year old with no teaching experience.

Most schools, if given the option, will most likely choose the more "American looking" teacher. Unfortunately, many people abroad think that you won't get a "real" English learning experience unless the person teaching the lesson looks like a stereotypical American. It is similar to how if you were going to choose a trainer at the gym you would most likely prefer to have the in-shape trainer work with you, as opposed to the trainer that looked like he could stand to do a little more running on the treadmill himself.

Naturally, how a trainer looks does not have anything to do with their knowledge regarding fitness, and how a teacher looks doesn't have anything to do with their knowledge regarding English, but some people, as human beings, get the impression that it does.

All that being said, this should definitely not discourage *anyone* (regardless of race or ethnicity) from trying to find work abroad. The reality is that most schools won't have the luxury of choosing among dozens of "perfect" candidates. If a school is in need of a teacher and you are available, they are likely to hire you.

Chapter 7: My Application Experience

"Life begins at the end of your comfort zone." – Neale Donald Walsch

Getting my positions in Spain and China didn't really require that much effort on my part after submitting my applications. Other than a simple phone interview, nothing else was required of me for either job. The application process I went through to get my job in Japan, however, was actually quite involved, and I'd like to share that experience so you can know what to possibly expect from your next potential employer (or AEON itself, if that is the route you choose to go).

After going online and filling out all of the forms and submitting all of the necessary documents (including an essay describing why I wanted to be a teacher) and being "accepted," I then had to go through the interview process. Unfortunately, AEON is a Japanese company, and as such they do not have any official locations in the United States. I actually had to go out to California to complete the two day interview at a hotel. Fortunately, I lived in Arizona, so it wasn't *that* big of a trek, but still involved a pretty high level of commitment on my part; buying a plane ticket, making a reservation at the hotel, renting a car, etc. Up to that point in my life, it was probably one of the most "adventurous" or "risky" things I'd ever done.

Every school/company is different, so don't expect them all to have a similar application process to AEON's. And don't be discouraged if applying to your desired school seems like a lot of work. Oddly enough, it's actually a good thing. The more work involved to apply not only means there will be fewer applicants to compete with, but also that the company is more likely to be on the up-and-up.

Anyway, the first day of the interview process involved two tests; grammar and spelling (yes, a spelling test, like you took back in the fourth grade). I suppose there are a number of reasons for this, but mainly they just want to know how much you know *about* English. Of course, you *speak* it, but do you *understand* it?

I went into the test feeling pretty confident. Even before deciding I wanted to teach English, I had always been fascinated by languages and had a deeper understanding of how language "works" than most people. However, that being said, I still did quite badly on the tests.

The spelling words were words that are commonly misspelled by native speakers. The following weren't the words I had to spell (I can't remember exactly the words they gave us), but ask yourself if you would be able to spell these words correctly if someone were to ask; camouflage, accommodate, conscientious, fiery, hygiene, occurrence, rhythm, and (perhaps the most difficult word in all of English) diarrhea. For fun, ask some of your friends how to spell these words and see how they do. I never got the results of my test, so I don't know how well (or poorly, rather) I did, but I'm sure I missed about half of them (and I'm sure having to stifle a laugh when the interviewer said "diarrhea" didn't help me much with landing a job either…).

The grammar test was quite challenging, too. It wasn't something simple like differentiating the usages of "there," "they're," and "their," but far more rhetorical (that is, of or relating to rhetoric) in nature. For example, one question I specifically remember was, "What is the difference between 'being envious' and 'being jealous?'" I wasn't sure at the time (I know now), so I just fumbled my way through some semblance of an answer. Another question was something to the effect of "What is the difference between 'used to' and 'would?'" And if I were to ask you, "What is the difference between 'I want to go too' and 'I want to go, too.'" (note the comma), What would you say? I remember for one of the questions I simply wrote, "I do not know. If a student were to ask me, so as not to confuse them with a vague, convoluted response, I would explain that I would look up the answer and tell them the next time I saw them." I figured it was better than nothing. Needless to say, I bombed the test, and any confidence I had had quickly left me like the air of a deflating balloon.

After the tests, the rest of the first day was spent teaching mock-lessons. Everyone was informed in advance that they would have to give an English lesson, where the other applicants would play the role of the students. Nobody was told *what* to teach, however. We were all able to freely choose whatever topic we liked. For a lot of people, this posed a little bit of a problem. I mean, what would *you* teach, if you were asked to give an English lesson? Fortunately for me, up to this point in time, I had done a little bit of studying of Japanese on my own and was somewhat familiar with the language. I knew, for instance, that in Japanese they don't have plural nouns. As such, pluralizing nouns poses a serious hurdle for Japanese students when learning English. So, I decided to make a lesson around that.

Up to that point in time, I had absolutely *no* experience teaching anyone anything in any kind of formal setting, let alone something as specific as 'when and how to properly pluralize nouns.' But all of the time I spent at home practicing in front of the bathroom mirror before heading off to L.A. paid off though, because I made it through my faux lesson feeling pretty confident. Looking back, my lesson was actually quite bad from a fundamental and structural stand point. However, the interviewers were well aware of the fact that most people coming in have almost zero experience teaching. What they're looking for is not so much *what* you teach, but *how* you teach it. What is your body language like? How do you project your voice? Did you call the students by their names? Were you smiling? These are all things that are absolutely *vital* to being a successful teacher (especially at a language training center like AEON).

So, if you're asked to give a lesson, don't worry if you think your content is "bad." Just remember that that's not what they're looking for. They are focusing on your personality and how you present yourself more than anything. They will teach you how to teach later.

Anyway, after everyone was finished and the first day was over, we were all told to wait in the lobby while the interviewers convened and decided who would come back for day two to take part in the one-on-one interviews. I felt pretty good about my lesson, but I knew I absolutely bombed the paper tests and wasn't very confident I'd be invited back. The 70+ of us passed the time slowly; talking about the tests (where I learned the differences between "envious" and "jealous") and how we felt about our chances of coming back. My confidence was even further shattered when I learned that out of all of the applicants, only *two* would be chosen for a position in Japan.

After a couple of hours, we were all called back and given manila envelopes with a slip of paper inside that determined our fates. I took a deep breath and opened mine to find that they had found me worthy enough to come back the following day. Some others I had befriended during the course of the day were not so "lucky" and had to go home feeling rejected. I, on the other hand, was over the moon. I had no idea what to expect for the interview, but I was confident because talking with people one-on-one was one of my strong points. The time I was given for my interview was 7:30 in the morning, which turned out to be the first one of the day. The early time didn't bother me at all because I had actually booked a room at the very same hotel the interview was being held, and I've always been a morning person, anyway.

I went back to my room and tried to think about all of the questions they might ask me, and tried to do a little more research about the company itself and even a little bit about Japan; its culture, history, current events, etc., so I could seem knowledgeable and ask some poignant questions.

I set my alarm for 5:00 in the morning, giving myself plenty of time to get ready. Even though the room where I'd do the interview was literally down the hall, I didn't want to be late. The next morning, after having showered, gotten dressed, and eaten breakfast, I still had about an hour before the interview, but decided to go wait outside the door of the interview room anyway. I am kind of a paranoid person, and I wanted to be sure the room hadn't disappeared in the middle of the night, or that something else equally implausible hadn't happened. At a little after 7:00, Henry, one of the interviewers came out of the room, surprised to see me. "Hi. Jeremy, right?" "Yes, sir. Good morning," I said. "You know our interview isn't until 7:30, right?" "Yes, but I just didn't want to be late." "Great, we can get started early then." He seemed pleased by my punctuality.

So, the interview began and after a few minutes I felt I was doing pretty well. One question he asked sort of tripped me up though, which was, "What would you do if you were to ask your Japanese manager for a couple days off, and they told you it was 'difficult?'" I gave the most diplomatic answer I could think of, "Well, I would sit down and talk with the manager about how we could adjust the schedule and figure out what was making the situation 'difficult' and try to resolve the issue together." Of course, my answer was "wrong." At the time I wasn't aware, but "difficult" is a word Japanese people use to mean essentially mean "no," but don't want to say "no" directly. In Japan, when you hear something might be "difficult," that means that you should give up on trying to accomplish whatever it is you're trying to do. Henry didn't seem too put off by my answer, though.

And just when I thought everything was going well, I was thrown for a complete loop. Henry then said, "Okay Jeremy. We are going to pretend you are a five year old Japanese student and I am going to give you an English lesson. After I finish, we are going to switch roles, and you are going to teach me the same lesson." "Sure, no problem," I said coolly, but was really panicking on the inside. Henry gave me his lesson then said, "Okay, I'm gonna go to my room and watch some TV for ten minutes or so while you prepare, and when I come back we can get started."

Those ten minutes flew by and I had no real idea what to do, but manged to somehow make my way through my lesson, trying my best to just do what Henry had done. One thing that I think impressed Henry was when I corrected his pronunciation. He was pretending to be a young Japanese boy, so instead of saying the word "passport" like a native English speaker would, he said, "pasupooto," which is actually the Japanese word for "passport." Thanks again to my knowledge of the Japanese language, I understood why he would say the word this way, and I went over the correct pronunciation with him a few times. Looking back it seems kind of funny to hear Henry, who was about 6'2" 200 lbs., say over and over "pasupooto" while I, in a sing-songy kind of tone, "No, Henry. It's 'passport.' 'Paaasssporrrt.'"

Anyway, the interview finished and I was told I could leave and that I would get a call a month or so later regarding their decision. I felt that Henry and I had developed a bit of a rapport, so I actually left feeling pretty confident. I flew back home with my fingers crossed, not knowing what I would do if I didn't get the job.

A couple months went by, and I had all but lost hope. "The least they could do is call to let me know I *didn't* get the job," I would mumble to myself every so often.

Then one day the phone rang. I picked up and Henry was on the other end. "Hey Jeremy," he said. "How are you?" We went through the motions of a typical conversation, all the while I was thinking he was just setting me up to break the bad news. Much to my surprise though, he was congratulating me on getting the job! I kept calm and cool as we finished our conversation and he told me he would be in touch with more details later, but as soon as I hung up the phone I literally jumped for joy. In just a few short months, I'd set off on what would be the start of accomplishing one of my dreams!

Again, that was just a story from my own personal experience. You won't necessarily have an experience similar to mine, but I think there are a number of things one who is going to take part in an extensive interview process can learn from it. I hope some of them prove useful to you.

Chapter 8: Dealing with Culture Shock

"Travel and change of place impart new vigor to the mind." – Seneca

One of the biggest problems teachers face when they arrive in their new homes is culture shock. One experiences culture shock when the culture surrounding them is so different from their own culture that they don't know how to handle themselves in various, typical day-to-day situations. Undoubtedly, you have heard of culture shock, but unless you have spent time outside of your native country, you've not likely experienced it first-hand.

How can you avoid 'the shock?' Well, when I went to Japan, I never experienced what I would consider a "culture shock." Sure, there were a few things that surprised me; like the sale of plastic "beauty nipples" in convenience stores, or vending machines with beer. But I never felt like I was in some kind of alien world where I couldn't function in society. Most of these differences were actually kind of cool (especially if you needed a drink on a hot day).

The best way to avoid culture shock, however, is to educate yourself as much as possible about the place you are going before you actually go there. Since I was a child, I had always been interested in Japan and knew quite a bit about the history and culture before actually going. As a result, I didn't suffer any anxiety when I was expected to eat with chopsticks, or take my shoes off before going into someone's home. I *was* a little surprised though during one trip to the dentist's office where the nurse explained to me that I needed to take off my shoes before stepping onto the "operating" floor. They really take their shoe-removing to the extreme over there.

I didn't experience any kind of culture shock during my time in Spain, either. I knew about its culture before going. So, when my host family and I wouldn't sit down to have dinner until 9:30 or 10:00 at night, I quickly acclimated. Though, that didn't seem to stop them from teasing me about how "early" Americans typically sup.

My experience with China is a little different story, however. Even though I educated myself well enough about the culture, the history, and the people before coming, sometimes no amount of preparation can get you ready for the real thing.

I'm sure everyone has heard stories about China, particularly the traffic, but it's hard to understand until you actually experience it yourself. I've almost been hit by a car a handful of times since coming, all while I was in the cross-walk with the little blinking man assuring me it was safe to cross! I also knew before coming here that people in China tend to talk a *little* loudly on the phone. But I had no idea as to just how loudly they talked until I came here and heard for myself first-hand... or is that "first-ear?"

Of course, none of these things are particularly "shocking." In fact, from a cultural perspective, these little "cultural quirks" can be kind of fun. But I feel it's important to be aware of the norms of the place you're going; not only for yourself, but out of respect for the native people. If you demonstrate knowledge of the country's culture (perhaps by using chop sticks, for instance, or avoiding a collision with an oncoming car by butt-sliding across the hood, Starsky and Hutch style), it often makes the people happy and lets them know that you are trying your best to assimilate.

One of the best ways to educate and familiarize yourself with what will be your new home's culture is to actually talk to someone who has been there. If you have a friend who has been to or used to live in China, for instance, they could be an untapped vein of knowledge and resources. Even if your friend is not native, talking to someone who has vacationed there or has passed through could provide valuable information. Just know, however, that you cannot prepare yourself for everything, but you should definitely make an effort before taking that flight. You must be flexible and understand that perhaps you are the one with the strange ideas.

Chapter 9: What to Expect When You're Expecting... to Go Abroad

"He who would travel happily must travel light." –
Antoine de St. Exupery

When people go abroad for the first time (whether it's just for travel, or more long-term), they're never quite sure what to expect. Unfortunately, I can't tell you what you should expect. I won't tell you something useless like, "expect the unexpected," though. In this chapter, I'll try my best to help you prepare for your unique experience.

The reality is that a lot of it depends on where you are going. That's why you should definitely educate yourself on the area in which you'll be living for the next year (or more!) of your life before going. Then, there won't be any surprises (or culture shock) when you arrive.

Here is a list of questions (and subsequent answers) people typically ask when they're bound for an overseas journey:

1. "What should I bring?"

The best piece of advice I (and Antoine de St. Exupery) can give you is to travel light. I think this pretty much applies *any* time one travels, but it especially applies in this case.

You have to realize that this is not a week-long trip. You're going to be *living* abroad, not vacationing. Assuming you're going to a modern, economically developed country, everything you would want or need to buy in your hometown will be available in some form or another in your new home, just with harder to read labels.

The last thing you want is to be lugging around three or four bulky suitcases in a foreign land where you likely don't speak or read the language very well (if at all). It might not seem like it would be an issue, but trust me. When you're rushing through the airport, trying to make heads or tails of the bus/subway map, asking someone for directions, etc., it just adds a little more stress to an already stressful situation. Plus, odds are you're going to have to do a bit of traveling/walking even after landing in your final destination. Hefting around heavy bags, especially after a long flight, is one of the last things you want to do.

Basically, I recommend just bringing clothes. When I worked in Japan, I had to wear a suit every day, so I made sure to bring a few (as a guy who is 6'4", I knew I wouldn't have much luck finding one that would fit me there). I also brought a few changes of casual clothes to wear when I wasn't working. I knew that if I needed more clothes, I could just buy them (though, finding appropriate sizes proved to be difficult at times).

Of course, you should definitely bring your laptop, iPad, the couple of textbooks you've been using to study the language, and so on, but there really isn't anything else you need that you won't be able to get once you settle in.

At the most, I recommend bringing just two suit cases. If you can get away with one though, that would be better. All you have to ask yourself while you're packing and cramming things into your suitcase is, "Can I buy this where I'm going?" If the answer is "yes," assuming it's not something terribly expensive, you should probably just leave it. Also, you want to make sure you have a lot of space available in your bags for your return trip home, because you're definitely going to pick up a lot of cool stuff that you'll want to take back and show everyone.

2. "Won't I miss my family and friends?"

Of course you will! But do you really want to give up the chance of a life time so you can watch reruns of *The Big Bang Theory* on Netflix with your pal Kyle, or go to that same ol' club with Carol that you went to last week, and the week before? No way! Besides, it's not like you're never going to come back. Everyone will still be there, and they'll be dying to hear tales of all of your travels.

Naturally, while abroad, you will miss some important things; weddings, the birth of a baby, graduations, etc., and it can be a bit of a bummer. But all of these things will be posted online for you to see, most likely in real time! It's not quite the same thing, but you can still share in people's happy moments. Just give them a call on Skype, or send a quick e-mail. Even when you're half-way across the world, you can easily feel connected with friends and family. So, don't worry about missing them. You'll stay in touch with the people who are truly close to you. In the meantime, you'll make new friends, some of which may even become as close to you as family. It definitely happened to me!

3. "How secure is the job I've been offered?"

Certainly before making all of the arrangements and finally heading abroad, you want to be confident that everything is on the up-and-up. There are definitely some shady organizations that want to take advantage of naive foreigners. That's why it's *your* responsibility to look into the company or person who hired you as much as possible before committing to anything. A simple Google search can probably reveal everything you need to know. But just remember, if something sounds too good to be true, it probably is.

4. "Will I make enough money to live comfortably?"

This is something that entirely depends on the job you take. Some jobs pay quite well, while others don't. Some don't even pay anything! (like my volunteer gig in Spain) This is something you'll definitely want to look into and determine before you sign that contract.

One of the first things you'll want to do is check out the exchange rate. When you see that by working for a school in Japan they'll pay you ¥230,000 a month, it certainly *looks* like a lot of money (all those zeroes!), but (as of the time of this writing) in USD it equates to about $2,100. Is that a lot of money? For some people it is, and for some people it isn't. But you also have to take other factors into account. Does your company pay for your room and board, or will it come out of your check every month? How much will their government take? (don't think you won't have to pay taxes) What's the cost-of-living where you'll be staying? Certainly basic necessities in a big city like Tokyo are much more expensive than they would be in a small town like

Nagasaki, so you'll need to factor that kind of information into your figuring.

Whether or not you can live comfortably mostly depends on you. I am basically a minimalist at heart; I do all of my own cooking, I *almost* never go shopping, I don't drink alcohol or smoke, and I only need the most basic of cell phone plans. So, in my case, ¥230,000 a month would be more than enough for me to live comfortably while also saving a little on the side.

Another thing to keep in mind is that exchange rates change. When I first went over to Japan in 2010, the exchange rate was down to about ¥75 to the dollar (I refer to them as the "golden days"). Needless to say, when I converted my salary to USD, I was making, what I considered to be, quite lot of money. Then, Prime Minister Shinzo Abe decided to go and "fix" the Japanese economy, and after a few months the rate skyrocketed to ¥100 to the dollar. My income had essentially been cut by 25%! Damn "Abenomics..."

I can tell you from personal experience that I've *never* had any trouble living comfortably in the places I've lived abroad. I've never known anyone who has had trouble, either. Certainly there are some people who may be irresponsible with money and run into problems, but for the most part schools (good schools) take care of their teachers. Why wouldn't they? They want to keep you for as long as possible. It costs a lot of money to find and hire teachers. So, they definitely want to make you happy, in hopes that you stick around and sign another contract when the time comes.

5. "Will I have adequate health care?"

Again, this is another detail (though a rather important one) that varies from school to school and program to program. Good programs will definitely provide their teachers with health care. Usually, it's not the *best* that an insurance company has to offer; just enough to cover the basics and satisfy visa application requirements. If someone offers you a position but won't provide health insurance, I suggest you thank them kindly for their offer, but look elsewhere for employment. If anything, it's indicative of how they will treat their teachers in other areas, as well.

Fortunately, I've never had the need for any kind of medical attention (though there were a couple times when I probably *should* have gone to the doctor and didn't). But if you're worried or nervous about it, I recommend picking up some international health insurance before heading off. You can talk to your current insurance company and get some kind of deal. Better safe than sorry.

6. "Will I have a social life?"

This is a tricky question, and I hate to be so indefinite in my answers to these questions, but it depends on the person.

Certainly, anyone who wishes to have a social life will find that meeting people and making new friends will be easier than it has ever been anywhere else back home.

The fact that you're a foreigner, particularly in Asian countries, almost instantly elevates you to celebrity status (perhaps a 'C' or even a 'B' lister). So, if you want to meet people, it is definitely within your power. In fact, even if you're the shy type, odds are people will come up and start talking to you! I can't tell you how many times I've been out and had people come up and introduce themselves, or ask if they could take a picture with me. In fact, a few weeks ago I was eating at a restaurant with some friends and the owner asked if he could take a picture with me. Perhaps he thought hanging a picture on the wall of himself with some random American guy would help give his establishment some street cred. I, of course, was more than happy to oblige, but not before my friend (who was then acting as my "agent") demanded he give us a

40% discount on our bill. He said, "Sure, no problem" and I was the hero for the night.

7. "There are *some* negative sides, right?"

Of course. You will certainly encounter numerous unpleasant things while you are living and working abroad, just like you experience and deal with a number of not-so-good things in your daily life now. Going abroad to teach isn't a vacation. It's work. And all of the baggage that typically comes along with work, and life in general, is included.

There is no getting around it. Teaching can be *extremely* frustrating. Even though I, overall, have thoroughly enjoyed my time living and working abroad, it certainly hasn't been without its days where I wanted to rip my hair out (as if it weren't falling out fast enough on its own), or just quit all together. I mean, you can only tell your students so many times that the word "clothes" (just like you told them last week, and the week before, and the week before that) is *not* pronounced as "close-is," before you snap.

And you may not get along with some of your co-workers, either. When I first came to China, I had a co-worker (another ESL teacher) who I absolutely *despised*, and he, likewise, me. We just couldn't work together. And if he was going to continue working at the school, I was going to leave. Fortunately, everyone else at the school realized too what a loser he was and he left (rumor has it that he couldn't get a police report that he needed in order to reapply for his visa. I suspect he had some kind of criminal history, to be honest). I still get giddy to this day when I walk by his old office and he's not there. In fact, thinking about it even now makes me smile. Hee-hee!

Chapter 10: Which Countries Are "the Best?"

"To travel is to discover that everyone is wrong about other countries." – Aldous Huxley

This is perhaps one of the most common questions I am asked; "Which country is the best for teaching English in?" Of course, as an English teacher, after admonishing them for ending a sentence with a preposition, I explain that it depends on what they mean by "the best."

Naturally, I can't discuss every possible destination. So, I will just list the more popular countries for teaching English along with some other relevant information.

Also, it should be noted that the information listed for each country is not necessarily 100% accurate. The "English language culture" around the world is constantly changing. So, the numbers and other information given here should not be taken as hard facts, as they are subject to change.

The given "Average monthly salaries" are simply rough estimations of what teachers can expect. Salaries will vary greatly depending on the school for which you are working and your experience as a teacher. You can make less than what I have listed below, or much more.

"Cost-of-living" will also very a great deal depending on which part of the country you will be living in. Cost-of-living in Beijing is much higher than the cost-of-living in Shaoxing, for instance. www.numbeo.com is a *great* website for finding information regarding cost-of-living (among other things) for your desired city.

I have also listed the "Academic year" for the countries below so you will know when the school year of that particular country begins. This information should not be so important for those of you who are looking to work at training centers, as they operate all year round and are likely to accept applications any time. If you wish to work at a public school, however, you will need to apply to a school before the school year starts. My recommendation is to apply a month or two before the school year is scheduled to begin.

All of that being said, I suggest you do your own research to find the most current information regarding your country and city of choice. At best, this information should just be used as a rough guide.

(All dollar figures are given in USD)

Brazil

> **Average monthly salary:** $1,000 - $1,500

> **Cost-of-living:** $800 - $1,000

Academic year: February – December

If your a fan of soccer and nature, then Brazil should definitely be on your radar of places to go. And thanks to the 2014 World Cup and the more recent 2016 Olympics, the desire to learn English is at a peak. Plus, who wouldn't want to have the chance to go to Carnival at least once in their life?

You don't stand to make too much money working in Brazil, but the adventures you'll have should more than make up for it.

Chile

Average monthly salary: $800 - $1,500

Cost-of-living: $800 - $1,000

Academic year: February – December

Chile is a place I've always wanted to go. There aren't too many places in the world where you can surf at the beach and then drive up to the mountains for some snowboarding in the same day. Plus, like many countries in South America, the demand for English is increasing and finding a job now should be easier than ever.

China

Average monthly salary: $1,000 - $3,000

Cost-of-living: $500 - $1,000

Academic year: September – July

The salary for teachers in China can vary (as you can see) quite drastically. As a teacher at a public school myself, I am at the higher end of the spectrum. Teachers at training centers and other private institutions will most likely make less. Room and board is often included with teaching jobs though, so your salary may not actually be as low as it seems at first glance.

Colombia

Average monthly salary: $1,500 - $1,700

Cost-of-living: $500-$900

Academic year: Some schools run from August – June, while others run from January to November (depends on the city)

I've never been to South America, but Colombia has always been a place I'd like to visit. The weather is great, and because of the low cost of living, teachers stand to save quite a bit of money.

Costa Rica

Average monthly salary: $1,400 - $1,700

Cost-of-living: $600 - $1,000

Academic year: February – November

It seems that as of late Costa Rica has become quite a popular destination among ESL teachers. Demand for teachers now is increasing, so finding a job shouldn't be too difficult.

Czech Republic

Average monthly salary: $700 - $1000

Cost-of-living: $600 - $900

Academic year: September – June

If medieval architecture is your thing, then you should definitely consider the Czech Republic. Prague is often touted as one of the most beautiful cities in Europe. And I hear the food there is quite good, too.

Dubai

Average monthly salary: $3,000 - $5,000 USD

Cost-of-living: $800 - $2,000

Academic year: September – June

If you were shocked by the average monthly salary, you shouldn't be. It shouldn't come as a surprise that the richest country in the world would pay its teachers so well. They don't just offer jobs to anybody in a tweed jacket with leather patches on the elbows, though. Five years of experience (minimum) is often required of applicants. Since I have surpassed the five year mark of teaching experience, I often think that the next place I'd like to go is Dubai. Maybe I'll see you there!

Ecuador

Average monthly salary: $400 - $600

Cost-of-living: $400 - 600

Academic year: October – July, or April – December (depends on the city)

Ecuador is one of the cheapest countries in which to live in South America. So, while the salary is quite low, the cost of living is too. You won't stand to make much money, but if you're a lover of nature, you should definitely consider Ecuador as one of your options.

Japan

Average monthly salary: $2,000 – $2,700

Cost-of-living: $1,000 - $1,500

Academic year: April – March (Japan has a trimester system, where each term is broken up by a long holiday. Their school year consists of approximately 200 days.)

I am quite partial to Japan, and definitely recommend it as my top teaching destination. From the culture to the food, Japan has it all. Not to mention, the people there are just some of the nicest people in the world. The amount of money you make (and spend) will vary quite a bit depending on where you live.

South Korea

Average monthly salary: $1,800 – $2,000

Cost-of-living: $1,300 - $1,600

Academic year: March – July

Times have certainly changed. South Korea used to be *the* place to go for teaching English. They offered the highest pay and best perks around. Now that other countries have stepped up their "trying to attract more English teachers" game, that's not the case anymore. That being said though, South Korea is still a great place to teach. You still stand to earn a nice salary (especially when you consider your room will most likely be paid for) and the facilities at most schools are quite state-of-the art. Plus, the level of respect teachers are shown in Korea has got to be one of the highest of any place you could go.

Spain

Average monthly salary: $1,800 – $2,000

Cost-of-living: $1,300 - $1,600

Academic year: September – June

Since I have personal experience teaching in Spain, I cannot recommend it enough. The country is beautiful, the people are great, and the food is *muy bueno* (gotta love the tapas!). Plus, just being in Europe itself is a plus. Got a three or a four day weekend? Just hop on a train and travel to another country you've been dying to go to.

Thailand

Average monthly salary: $800 – $1,500

Cost-of-living: $400 - $600

Best time to apply: May – February

I've heard great things about teaching in Thailand, and I've heard not so great things. The country itself is beautiful, and if you find a high enough paying salary you can definitely save quite a bit of money while you're there, since the cost-of-living is so low. Some schools treat their teachers better than others, so I recommend researching your school's reputation in the ESL community thoroughly before signing any contracts.

I've been to Thailand on vacation though, and had a blast. I'd definitely recommend it to those of you who are simply looking to have a good time. Here's a picture of me taking a bite out of Tony the Tiger in Puhket.

Turkey

> **Average monthly salary:** $2,000 – $2,500

> **Cost-of-living:** $1,300 - $1,700

> **Academic year:** September – June

Turkey isn't often a country that comes into people's minds when they are trying to figure out where they want to teach English, but I think it's definitely worth considering. With a mix of the Middle East and Europe, you'll definitely find an interesting bit of culture here. Plus, you could maybe even check out one of their famous(?) oil wrestling matches (Google it) in person, and who wouldn't want to see that?

Vietnam

> **Average monthly salary:** $1,300 – $2,000

> **Cost-of-living:** $600 - $900

> **Academic year:** August – June

Vietnam is another country where a lot of teachers go when they want to not only have a great experience, but make a little money while they do it. The salaries offered in Vietnam can be quite high, while the cost-of-living is quite low.

Chapter 11: What Qualifications Do I Need?

"People don't take trips, trips take people."
– John Steinbeck

One of the most common misconceptions people have is that in order to teach abroad you have to have a teaching degree, or have studied English in college. While it certainly *helps* to have an English/teaching background, it is definitely *not* a requirement.

I studied business in college, and other than the fact that I spoke English natively, I had almost nothing official to demonstrate any kind of proficiency or ability to actually *teach* it. In fact, I had basically *zero* teaching experience when I was hired to teach in Japan. So, just know that almost regardless of your background, as long as you are a native English speaker you should be able to find a job *some*where. The more credentials/qualifications you have, however, the more opportunities you'll have. Most countries, especially now that there are more and more people going to teach abroad, are getting pickier when it comes to the teachers they hire.

As I mentioned before, an English degree isn't required by most schools. However, a college degree *is* an absolute must for most places.

TESOL and TEFL

Something else that will open a lot of doors in terms of employment opportunities is a TESOL (Teaching English to Speakers of Other Languages) or TEFL (Teaching English as a Foreign Language) certification.

As far as I know, they are basically the same and are equally accepted by all schools (though it couldn't hurt to check if your country of choice has a preference for one over the other). I got my TESOL certification through www.ontesol.com. I took the online, 100-hour course, but there are many different options. Odds are there is even a physical school in your area that you can go to in order to get certified to teach English as a second language.

If you're really serious about teaching abroad, I recommend at *least* getting a basic 100-hour certification. And I also recommend going the online route. Having the certification is more of a formality than anything (in my experience). In reality, you won't learn much from the course (I certainly learned very little from mine). Everything you need to know will basically come from experience. But it is something that many schools require, so I would recommend to anybody to just take the cheapest, easiest route in acquiring your certification. Many programs also provide assistance in finding placement after completing their course. Though, beware of promises that sound too good to be true. No company, for instance, can *guarantee* placement, and you should be weary of any that do.

I mentioned before that I didn't have any experience or qualifications for teaching before being hired by AEON. I decided, in order to prepare myself and be the best teacher I could be, to get a TESOL certification, even though it wasn't actually a requirement of AEON. After getting certified, I had for a number of years considered it a waste of time (and money!), since I didn't need it for my jobs in Japan or Spain, and nothing (absolutely *nothing!*) I learned from the course helped me in the classroom (frankly, I think the whole TESOL/TEFL industry is just a big scam). But when I applied for my current job here in China, a TESOL/TEFL certification was required, and I was glad that I had done the course because I wouldn't have been hired without it. So, even if you don't need a TESOL/TEFL certification for your desired school now, I recommend getting certified anyway. It certainly couldn't hurt to be able to write it on your résumé, and you never know where you'll want to go next. It might be a requirement there. Plus, getting certified can take months, and you may not have the time to finish a course before an offer comes and goes.

Experience is obviously also very important. Some positions (the really good ones) require years of experience. Fortunately, if you have no experience, most schools are still willing to hire you. If you're going to work at a training center, the school will most likely train you. When I first arrived in Japan, before I went to the actual school where I'd be working, I went through quite a rigorous two-week training course that taught me *how* to teach "the AEON way." You should find out if the program you choose offers training for their newly hired teachers as well.

To put it in a nutshell, all you *really* need to teach English abroad is to be a native English speaker, but a college degree along with a TESOL/TEFL certificate and some actual classroom experience will go a *long* way in finding a really good position.

Chapter 12: But I Don't Speak the Language

"To have another language is to possess a second soul."
–Charlemagne

Another thing people often fret over is the fact that they don't speak any other languages. When I told people I was going to Japan, one of the first questions I was asked was, "How are you going to teach over there? You don't speak Japanese." Of course, at the time I didn't speak Japanese, but I wasn't worried. And if you don't speak Japanese, Chinese, Spanish, Thai, or whatever, you don't have to worry, either.

Some schools may require that you speak the students' native language, but a *vast* majority of schools don't care one way or the other. In fact, when I was living and working in Japan, speaking Japanese at the school was "forbidden." And the reality is that most schools actually prefer teachers who don't speak anything *but* English!

The idea is that schools want their teachers speaking English with their students at all times, to help give them a more 'immersive experience.' Their philosophy is that it's not a place for *you* (the teacher) to practice *your* language skills. Basically, they don't want you gabbing it up with students in their native language.

And as far as life *outside* of the school goes, I've never found not knowing the language particularly troublesome. In fact, I have found the *opposite* to be quite true on many occasions. For instance, I recently went to the bank to transfer some money from my account here in China to my account in the U.S. My Chinese is certainly nowhere near good enough to read the necessary documentation or communicate to the clerk exactly what I am looking to do. So, my Chinese friend that I dragged along ended up basically doing everything for me (naturally, I treated her to lunch after we had finished). And you'll find that there are many other situations where your friends will just take over for you, because there is basically no other choice. Naturally, I do not encourage you to use this as a reason to not learn the language.

The reality is that most people around the world study English in school, and not only can most people speak it well enough, they will jump at the chance to do so! Since I travel to different countries in order to *learn* languages, I often found this to be quite frustrating, actually. I can't tell you how many times I've asked someone in their native language something like, "How do I get to the post office from here?" Only to have them respond in English.

So, if you don't speak the language, don't worry. You shouldn't have any real trouble or problems either at or outside of work. **Chapter 13: What's a Good Amount of Time to Spend Abroad?**

"Not all those who wander are lost." – J.R.R. Tolkien

Before making the move to Japan, my original plan was to stay two years (three at the *most)*. Since my main goal was simply to learn the language, I thought this would give me more than enough time and plenty of opportunities to do other cool things, as well.

Most contracts with schools are initially for one year, with an option to renew (if the school likes you). So, theoretically, one could work five, ten, or even twenty years at a school if they chose to do so. The JET program, however, is different. They will only allow you to teach with them for five years. Then, you have to go off and find something else. I'm not quite sure what they theory behind that is. I haven't heard of any other program that has a limit like that.

On average, though, most teachers who go abroad only spend a little over a year before deciding to call it quits. Some people, of course, get homesick, or decide that teaching isn't really there thing and may even leave before finishing their first year. A girl I trained with at

AEON ended up quitting after only a few weeks, as a matter of fact, due to being homesick. And some people just feel like they want to take a break from their life back home for a year or so and try to figure some things out.

Personally speaking, I think one year is way too short. It sounds like a long time, especially before you actually head off, but the time just flies by and before you know it, your first year will be coming to an end and you'll have to decide whether or not you want to renew that contract and stick around.

The reason I say that one year is so short is because the first six months, at the very *least*, are spent just acclimating to your new environment. I only started to feel *slightly* comfortable in Japan after about half a year, and that was only *slightly*. I was just starting to feel like I was getting the whole teaching thing down (if you have no experience, believe me, it takes a while before you get used to it; years, really). I was picking up the language a little bit and had a pretty good daily routine down; wake up, study, go to the gym, go to work, go grocery shopping, go home, study, sleep. I finally felt comfortable with the neighborhood and knew where all of the important things were; post office, grocery store, ATM, etc. After six months though, I still hadn't found a "real friend," someone I

would want to call on weekends to hang out with. I had
some developing relationships in the works, but nothing
substantial. I didn't really develop a good group of
friends until about a year and a half of living in Japan.

That's why I can't imagine why anyone would want to
leave after only one year. That's when everything starts
to get good! You've developed a routine at work and it's
much easier than it was initially, you have good friends
to spend time with, you get to know the locals and can
even chat a little bit as you commute to and from work.
But that's when most people choose to leave; after
doing all of that work and just when your life would
start to reach some sort of normalcy. Crazy!

I said earlier that I had planned to stay two or three
years, originally. But I found that two years was *still*
too short. Even after two years, I still didn't feel like I
had completely settled into my new life in Japan. The
number of things to learn and do is truly mountainous
and cannot possibly be done in just two short years. I
understand that this may not be an option for everyone,
but if you really want to have a good experience, I
recommend staying for at *least* two, but three would be
better. I ended up staying for nearly five! The crazy
thing is that I could have stayed longer, but I wanted to
go out and explore other places before "getting

trapped." Maybe that's why JET has their five year limit...

Chapter 14: How to Make the Most out of Living in my New Home

"A mind that is stretched by a new experience can never go back to its old dimensions."
– Oliver Wendell Holmes

In this chapter, I will discuss how to make living in your new home as comfortable and enjoyable as possible. I'll give some advice as to what I think you should do, and even discuss a little bit about my personal experiences.

One of the first things you're going to want to do is make friends. When you arrive at your new home, you basically know *zero* people. So, initially, when you have some free time you are going to be spending a lot of it by yourself. That, of course, is not very fun or exciting. So, making friends is one of the best ways to not only cure any kind of boredom, but also to get to know the area and learn about the culture first-hand.

What's the best way to make new friends? My recommendation, and it's going to sound a little strange, is to join a boxing gym. Yeah, that's right, champ, a boxing gym.

When I was still quite new to my home in Nagasaki, I would go jogging after work. In addition to just being some good ol' fashioned exercise, it also allowed me to explore my new home and kind of get to know the area a little better. At first, because I was scared I might get lost. I never ran so far as to let my building out of my sight. As time went on, however, I grew bolder and would venture down new streets and alleys. One day, I happened to run past a boxing gym and could see nine or ten people inside training. I actually kick-boxed back home for a number of years, so I had some experience, but I had never done just straight *boxing* (they are quite different, kick-boxing and "regular" boxing). I thought this would be a great way to get to know some people. As odd as it may sound, people you meet at a boxing gym are some of the nicest people in the world. I had been living in Japan for about only three months and didn't speak the language well at all, but decided to go inside anyway.

As expected, everyone was really nice and I ended up joining. Afterward, I made visiting the boxing gym a regular part of my weekly routine (Monday, Tuesday, Wednesday, Friday 9:30-10:30; Saturday 7:30- 9:00).

I stayed a member of the gym up until I left Japan (so for over four years) and can honestly say I met some of my best friends there, some of with whom I am still in contact today. The owner of the gym took a real liking to me and basically thought of me as a son (even more so than his *actual* son). He'd invite me over for dinner, or we'd go out together from time to time. I even got to know his family quite well. Joining the gym was one of the best decisions I have ever made.

Just as a side note, I even took part in an actual match where I won by K.O. in the first round; just another experience I wouldn't have had otherwise. As an added bonus, I even got paid for my appearance! So, technically I can say that I was, at one point, a professional boxer.

Me just before making my boxing debut.

Of course, boxing isn't everyone's thing, but you should definitely find some club or activity you can join and meet local people, whether it's yoga, basketball, judo, or flower arranging. Your co-workers at school would be more than happy to help you if you were to ask.

This next one is obvious, but you're definitely going to want to do a bit of traveling while you're abroad. How many people would love to see Mt. Fuji? A lot, right? Now, how many people will actually *go* and see it? Probably not very many. And it's not because they don't want to. It's just because Mt. Fuji is on the other side of the world (for most people). When you're living in your new home, popular tourist destinations may just be an hour or two away from your very own door! Take advantage of this amazing situation. Like I said, this seems like a no-brainer, but you'd be surprised by how often foreign teachers don't take in all of the sights. Currently I'm living in China, and in a couple weeks I'll be going to see the terracotta warriors in Xi'An and then the Great Wall. They're just a couple hour's flight away! How lucky am I? I definitely need to see this stuff now, because odds are I won't have another chance any time soon.

Chapter 15: Making Extra Money on the Side

"You don't have to be rich to travel well."
– Eugene Fodor

If you think the money you're being paid by your school isn't enough, odds are you'll want to find a way to earn a little extra cash.

There aren't many options for a foreigner. Your visa likely will not allow you to work as anything but a teacher at your school. And even if it were possible, nobody would be likely to hire you for another job simply because of all of the paperwork/hassle it would be, tax-wise.

Fortunately, there is at least one way you can easily make some scratch on the side; teaching English! As if it wasn't obvious enough…

Unfortunately, most training centers will likely have a policy against this, which is understandable. If you teach someone privately, you're basically "stealing" a potential customer from your very own school. So, it's easy to see why they frown upon this.

Naturally, the school won't have any idea what you're doing after you go home. So, if you feel like you want to teach a couple of lessons on the weekend, I say go for it. Just make sure that your students understand that they shouldn't go around telling everyone about your arrangement, or it will likely make its way to your boss.

Another way to make an honest buck is to do some translation work on the side. Of course, you'll need to know the language, but it can be a great way to make some dough (I wonder how many synonyms I can use for the word "money" by the end of this chapter…). When I was in Japan, I translated some documents for Mitsubishi, which has a plant in Nagasaki, and got about 500 smackers for one day's work; not too bad.

-Finding students

You may be wondering about the best way to go about finding students to teach privately. This can be tricky, depending on your working situation.

If you're working at a public school, there shouldn't be any problem teaching classes on the side, and your fellow teachers will likely know someone and could introduce you. You may even be able to give lessons to the other teachers! (It's hard to charge them a lot, though… and as a result won't generally be worth it.)

You could also find a community center or some place locals congregate and post a flier/note on a bulletin board advertising your services. This seems like a lame, old-fashioned way to do it, but it's definitely effective.

For teachers of training centers, such options aren't usually available. That isn't to say that finding private students is impossible, though.

After you have established a group of friends, ask them if they might know anyone who wants to study English. Odds are they will, and your friends can introduce you.

The reality is you won't have to actually put much work into finding your own students. By just being a foreigner, you are effectively advertising constantly *wherever* you go; like a walking, talking billboard. Sometimes people might even just stop you on the street and ask if you can give them (or their children) lessons. This is especially true in Asian countries where competition for junior high and high school placement is quite fierce, and parents (especially the "tiger moms") are always on the lookout for a way to get a one-up on the competition.

In fact, true story, a few days ago as I was skating my way home from the grocery store and a middle aged man waved me down from the street, "Ni hao, ni hao!" he said. I thought for sure he was going to be some weirdo that wanted to practice his English, or just shake hands with me (yes, sometimes people do come up to me out of nowhere and want to shake hands), but it turned out he was a professor at a local college, and he wanted me to teach his son English. He didn't speak any English himself, but fortunately my Chinese is good enough now to communicate and understand this kind of basic information (another good reason to learn the language; potential jobs!). We exchanged numbers, and now we're working on setting something up.

Speaking from my own experiences, however, I have never put much effort into finding private students. I've had a few throughout my ESL career, but for the most part I don't think they're worth it, and I'll discuss why.

Setting up times and dates and trying to work your schedule around classes can be a lot more work than you might think, especially if the person you're dealing with doesn't speak English (and your foreign language skills ain't so good either).

Also, figuring out *where* you're going to teach is another hassle. I definitely do *not* recommend having them come to your home, or you going to theirs. You'll have to find some place that is convenient for the both of you. So, your best bet would likely be a coffee shop that is nearby. But you probably won't have a car, and unless you're cool and get around on a skateboard like me, you'll not likely have a convenient way to get from place to place, and you may have to spend a good 15-20 minutes just *getting* to your destination, which would easily add up to over a half hour in total time spent commuting.

And there is absolutely *no* way your class will end on time. If your class is set to finish at 4:00, what are the chances you think you will head out of the café and start making your way home at 4:01? Your private lesson student will try to milk all of the English learning out of you as possible. You would be surprised by how hard it can be to end a class that doesn't officially finish with a bell (if you're bold, you could bring your own little timer to your lessons). You'll want to leave, but at the same time, you won't want to appear rude. You can easily end up staying 5-10 minutes (or more!) after your class has officially ended, and during that time you're essentially working for free. That's definitely not a good feeling.

An ultra conservative estimate of the amount of time you'll spend, in total, teaching a one hour private lesson is an hour and twenty five minutes (and that's not even counting the time you spent *before* the lesson in preparation). It could easily be more. Fifteen or twenty wingwangs an hour for your lesson may initially *seem* like an okay deal, but when you factor in the total time you spent on it, you'll probably come to the conclusion that it's just not worth it.

If you do decide you want to take on some private students, try to find *multiple* students and set up their classes to run back-to-back (or, better yet, teach them all in a group). Then the half-hour travel time could be cut in half (or a third) from an "average time spent commuting per number of classes" point of view. Commuting for thirty minutes doesn't seem so bad when you're going to teach three classes instead of one.

If you're going to teach multiple classes, I also recommend making your official lesson time fifty minutes, and not a whole hour. This way you can set up your classes to start *on* the hour, while giving you ten minutes to prepare for your next student after your previous lessons has finished. Also, when the student you just finished class with tries to milk extra English time out of you, it doesn't feel so bad because you still have some time before your next class starts, and you wouldn't be doing much of anything with that time anyway. It is also the perfect excuse for getting them to leave; "I'd love to sit and talk more with you Rikichika, but I have another class to teach, so I'll see you next week!"

If you do decide just to take on one student, make sure that it is worth your time. In Japan, I had one class I taught for fifty minutes (not an hour) where I was paid 10,000 Yen (that's over 100 clams U.S.), and the commute was only 10 minutes. I did, however, often spend time after the class socializing, but seeing as how the pay along with my relationship with the students was so good, I was more than happy to do so. In fact, after our lessons we would often go out for dinner together, and we would mostly end up speaking Japanese, which turned out to be a great lesson for *me*.

Another reason I never got into taking on private students is that my time is much more valuable than what most people are willing to offer me in exchange for it. I would rather study Japanese/Chinese/Spanish for an hour and a half than sell that hour and a half for a measly 20 greenbacks. Needless to say, if I had to guess, I probably won't end up taking on that college professor's son as a student. It never hurts to hear an offer, though. We'll see what happens.

Anyway, everyone's situation and philosophy is different. If you think you want to find some private students, just try to keep my advice in mind when doing so.

Chapter 16: Other Tips and Words of Advice

"Oh the places you'll go." – Dr. Seuss

In this chapter, I'm going to attempt to dispense some wisdom or little "tips" that will help make your stay abroad much more enjoyable.

1. Don't do anything "bad"

This may seem like an obvious/unnecessary "tip," but let me explain. Odds are, wherever you decide to go, you will either be the only foreigner (or perhaps one of a few) in your area. This means that everyone in the community will quickly know your face and be able to recognize you *immediately*. So, if you decide to go out one night and you happen to drink a little too much and cause a ruckus, finding and identifying you will be easy for the authorities. The only description they'll need of you is "the foreign guy/gal," and they'll be knocking on your door that same night.

A funny thing happened to me while I was living in Japan. Some rich, business-type guy found out his wife was stepping out on him with a foreigner who lived in the area. Not knowing any other information about the foreigner other than that he was a blonde English teacher, he immediately set out to find him. I happened to be a blonde English teacher (one of only a few in the area) and the guy immediately suspected me. He actually even hired guys to trail me, in an attempt to "catch us." I eventually explained to one of his associates that they had the wrong guy and that not only did I have no idea what they were talking about, but that I had never even *met* his wife, let alone given her any "private lessons." Anyway, I'm not quite sure how the whole thing ended. They must have found the actual guy, or just realized that it wasn't me, because I didn't see or hear anything from them afterward.

Odds are something as "sitcomy" as this won't likely happen to you, but just know that everyone in your town will know who you are, and you have to be on your best behavior because you won't be able to get away with anything, and you never know who might be watching you.

2. Find a tutor to teach you the language

I know I have said it numerous times already, but learning the language of the country you're in is absolutely essential if you want to make the most out of your experience. In addition to just making you a better teacher, it will help you in countless other ways as well; from making friends, to going shopping, even to calming down hired goons.

If you're like most people (and me), you don't have the mental fortitude to do it all by yourself. That's why I recommend finding a tutor. The staff at your school should be able to help you find one. My current Chinese teacher was actually my co-worker's personal trainer; someone I likely never would have been able to find on my own.

It's okay if you don't *master* the language, but you should be able to speak at least a *little*. I'm sure you'd regret it if you were to spend a year or two in Cuba, and the only thing you could express was that *tienes un gato en tus pantalones.*

In addition to helping you out with the language, your tutor will also be able to introduce you to new people and teach you about the culture. My Japanese teacher ended up becoming one of my closest friends. She also introduced me to many people that ended up becoming really close friends. I'm sure if I had never met and taken classes with her, my time in the land of the rising sun wouldn't have been nearly as bright.

3. Don't spend too much time hanging out with other foreigners

I find that this often seems like the most strange (and difficult) "rule" for most ex-pats to abide by. I could never understand why people would travel half-way around the world, just to hang out with other ex-pats. By doing that, you're missing 95% of the whole 'being abroad experience!' If you have a couple friends who are non-natives like yourself, that's okay, but put some effort into making friends who are locals.

I've always made a conscientious effort not to befriend non-natives during my times abroad. That isn't to say that I'm rude to other foreigners by any means, but I just choose not to associate with them. In fact, I even go so far as to try and not associate with *anyone* who speaks or wants to learn to speak English (local people included). At work, of course, I have no problem with it, but when I'm off the clock, I'm not going to be anyone's English-teaching pal. You'll find that a lot of people will want to be your friend *just* so they can practice their English. I've always *hated* that. It feels like I am being used. Some people might think this is extreme, but now I can speak Japanese and Spanish, and I'm picking up Chinese pretty quickly. So, I'd say it's worth it, even if you may come across as unfriendly or anti-social.

4. Don't date students or associate with them outside of the class

Most schools have a policy against dating students. I don't mean public schools, of course. Naturally, the junior high and high schools don't want the teacher in his/her mid-twenties or thirties dating any of their teenage students (and neither do the local authorities). I'm talking about private schools and training centers.

It's important to separate your professional and personal life. If you start mixing them, it can cause quite a bit of trouble. If your students are adults, there's no doubt you'll have a student you think is cute, and there will be plenty of opportunities to go out with that person. I don't recommend it. In addition to violating my "associating with natives that speak/want to learn English" rule, it just cannot end well for you in the long run.

How have your relationships worked out up to now? Unless you're married, it's pretty to safe to say all of them have failed. And that's okay. But the problem with dating students is that that relationship will also fail (statistically speaking), and it will undoubtedly affect your school's bottom line. And if you're costing your school money, do you think they'll want to keep you around? Your ex is definitely not going to want to continue going to the school if you're there (there goes at least one contract). Plus, there will likely be rumors and you might develop a bad reputation with the other students, as your now ex-boyfriend/girlfriend will likely have friends at the school who might decide you're a bad person and quit the school, as well.

As a foreigner, you'll *definitely* have a lot more opportunities to hook up with someone of the opposite sex (or same sex, if that's you're thing) than you currently do at home, but if you do feel like you want a boyfriend/girlfriend, my advice is to try and find one outside of the school.

5. Easiest way to be a "good" teacher

In order to be a good teacher, what do you think is one of the most important things you can do? Think about it for a second. It's really quite simple… Give up? Okay, I'll tell you; remembering your students' names (and then using them!).

It's hard to imagine, but when you, the cool foreign teacher, call out a student's name directly in class or when walking down the hall, it means the *world* to that student. Before I started teaching, I never really gave calling people's names much thought. But when you're walking down the hall and you see Hiroyuki looking down at the floor as he trudges on to his next class and you say, "Hey, Hiroyuki!" it will make his day. I actually used to get in trouble when I first started working in Japan because I just could not remember (and as a result, could not *use*) my students' names. I tried to claim that I had a mild case of prosopagnosia, but my boss wasn't buying it. In my defense though, I had, in one class, students named Ai, Aya, Aiko, Ayako, and Akiko. They also liked to sit next to each other. I think they did it on purpose…

My experience in China, however, has been *much* easier because students here adopt English names. So, remembering a Bill or a Peter is much easier than remembering a Wang Fei Fei or Wu Yan Hui.

Either way, the reason that remembering your students' names is so important is that it will help build a rapport with them, and is one of (if not *the)* easiest things you can do that will make you more successful as a teacher.

6. Create new social media accounts

There is an extremely high likelihood that your students will ask you about your Facebook, Twitter, Instagram, Google+, WeChat, QQ, or MySpace account (well, maybe not MySpace) and want to be your "friend."

In Japan, I made the mistake of giving some students my Facebook account. As you can imagine, if you give it to one student, by the end of the week the entire school population will know it, and you'll be bombarded with friend requests and inundated with annoying messages (like, "Are you from?") that you will (if you're like me) feel obligated to answer. It will end up feeling like a second job, but with no pay…

That's why I recommend making new "country-specific" accounts. It can be hard to tell a student "no," when they ask to be your "friend." If you say no, they might feel embarrassed and then it could be awkward for them in class. If you make a new account, however, you can give it out freely, while still being able to keep your "real" life private. If they ask you, "Do you have Facebook?" Just say, "Before coming to [name of country you're in] I didn't, but I just made one. You can add me!" and they'll be thrilled to have a foreign friend. And since you told them you just made it, they likely won't find it suspicious you don't have many other friends on your account.

In addition to keeping the annoying factor to a minimum, it will also be a big help professionally. Most people who teach abroad are relatively young and are likely to have photos that they would rather not have their students see (like that one of you at the frat party totally killing that beer-bong). While developing and maintaining good relationships with your students, it's important to keep your personal and professional life separate. The amount of time/energy/trouble this one tip alone will save you is definitely worth the price you paid for this book.

7. Learn to sing a song in your students' language

This may seem like a strange one, but I guarantee learning to sing a song in your students' language will come in *way* more handy than you would normally think, especially if you're going to Asia, where karaoke is king.

In addition to helping you learn a little bit of the language, I can guarantee that your students will be blown away if you belt out a song they all know.

This piece of advice is particularly useful for those of you who will be teaching at a training center. One big part of working at a training center is, as I've mentioned before, developing good relationships with students. As such, your school will likely throw a lot of parties or just have informal nights out with students. Karaoke is becoming more and more popular all over the world and there is a good chance you'll be invited to go sing. Of course, your students will love to hear you sing their favorite songs in English, with your "perfect pronunciation," but if after rocking the house with Taylor Swift's "Shake it Off," you can sing a popular song from their country, they'll be amazed. Even if you butcher the lyrics/pronunciation, they'll just be happy that you tried and love you for it.

This is not only useful for when you're out with students, though. This ability will no doubt come in handy when you're just out with your friends. I can't tell you how many times I brought the house down in Japan with "Linda Linda" by The Blue Hearts (YouTube it). I had about four Japanese songs in my karaoke repertoire that would always kill. The effort to learn the songs is definitely worth the reward (the other three were "Playback Part 2" by Yamaguchi Momoe, "Nantokanare" by Furuido, and "Namida no kissu" by The Southern All-Stars, in case you were wondering. Check those out as well).

The mic was hot, but my ears were cold

If you're thinking, "I'm too shy to sing," or "There's no way I could sing in front of a room of people," then maybe teaching abroad isn't for you. You have to get over being shy, and singing in front of an audience isn't much different than teaching a classroom full of people. They're both essentially performances.

It doesn't have to be a difficult song. Choose something easy. In fact, I was invited out to a wedding a couple weeks ago here in China and, I'm not exactly sure why, the bride and groom (whom I had never actually met before) asked me to sing a song. The only song I knew was a children's song called *Liang Zhi Laohu*, (The Two Tigers) to the tune of *Frere Jaques*. I invited a couple kids on stage with me and we all sang together, and everyone seemed to get a kick out of it. The idea of a blonde haired, blue-eyed American singing in Chinese was enough for them to be impressed by anything that came out of my mouth in Chinese, even if it was a silly nursery rhyme. I'm currently in the process of learning a more age-appropriate song though, so I can sing something *good* the next time the opportunity comes up (which it undoubtedly will).

8. Develop a routine

One of the biggest problems new teachers face is establishing some kind of regularity in their new lives. After being dropped off at a completely different part of the planet, it is hard to acclimate, regardless of how much you prepare.

That's why I recommend all teachers try to develop a routine as soon as they can. It may not be possible during the first couple weeks though, as *everything* is new and you still don't really know your very own schedule, let alone the schedules of other people/places.

After you do have a bit of an understanding of your new surroundings and what your work-load/schedule is like, then you can try to make a basic routine to start living by.

As corny as it sounds, it is best to actually write down this schedule, as it will make you more likely to stick to it (it's a psychological thing).

Do your best to fill out a schedule for every day of the week. Write down when you're going to wake up on days you have work and days you have off. Write down what time you're going to have breakfast, lunch, and dinner. Write in the time for when you're going to start and finish studying. Think about what day and time you are going to go grocery shopping or train at that boxing gym I told you to join.

As you live in your area longer and longer, you'll discover more things to do and places to go, and you can keep adding to your routine.

Naturally, it is okay to diverge from your routine. Maybe you were planning on having lunch at home at 12:00 in the afternoon, but you ran into a friend and went out to lunch that day. Any change you make is okay, as long as you *had* a plan to begin with.

I think that developing a routine is so important because otherwise you won't really know what to do with yourself when you're not working. Even if you work eight or nine hours a day, you will find that you still have a lot of time to yourself when you get off work.

Now, in your home country, you probably have some routine developed for after work/school where you give your best friend a call, go to the gym, watch some TV, have dinner, and then hit the sack, but many of the things you do in your free time now won't really be options (at least not right away) when you find yourself in your new home. You won't have friends to call, and you probably won't understand (or like) what's on TV. If you don't try to get into some routine, you'll likely just spend your time watching cat videos on YouTube all day, which, although very entertaining, is just a colossal waste of time.

With my current job in China, my total work time is less than 15 hours a week (unbelievable, right?). Oh, the free time I have! As a result, I had to find many different ways to effectively use my time, like writing this book, or picking up the harmonica. After writing down my own routine, I felt much more comfortable and "in control." I felt like I had a life and that I wasn't just some long-term tourist with nothing to do but twiddle my thumbs (though, I do still enjoy the occasional cat video).

Unfortunately, I've met quite a few ESL teachers who didn't make an effort to develop a routine on their own, and I think it may have made their experiences abroad less fulfilling, like my old AEON co-worker who quit just after two weeks because she was homesick. If she had found something to do with her time, she may have had a much different experience.

Naturally, over time, you will develop a routine just by living your day-to-day life, and you won't have to rely on the one you wrote. But after just entering the country, I promise it will make your life much easier (and better!).

9. Become a regular somewhere - The Bantan Story

If possible, I recommend finding a nice café or any quiet place to frequent. The more you visit a particular place, the more likely you'll be to meet people and make new friends. Some people might be too shy to start up a conversation with you at first, but after they see you a couple times, they will eventually work up the courage to introduce themselves. The same goes for you, too, of course.

I said that I recommend a café or a quiet place because the customers who go there will likely be more "mellow" and "nicer" than those you'll find at most bars. Bars can be okay, too, but they're often too loud to allow for any decent conversation (making building a relationship a bit more difficult), and you're also more likely to find disagreeable patrons.

On my walk home from work every night, I would always take the same route and pass by the same stores, bars, and cafés. And five nights a week I would walk by a quaint little café called Bantan. The owner, whom I could see through the large front window, was a pleasant looking, older lady in her mid-60's. On some nights, she'd have a room full of customers (since it was quite small, eight or nine people would constitute "being full") and on other nights she'd have none. And on those nights I could see her just sitting at the counter staring off into nothing, or reading a magazine. At this particular time, my Japanese wasn't very good, but I thought that she seemed kind of lonely and I wanted to talk to her. I "chickened out" a couple times, always saying, "Next time she's by herself I'll go in." I did eventually muster up the courage to go in when she was alone one night (I certainly wasn't going to go in when there were other customers) and sit down at the bar. She didn't seem *too* surprised to see a 6'4" American walking through her door, and she politely asked, "Nan ni nasaimasu ka?" (What would you like?) I ordered something, and seeing as there was really nothing else to do, we made small-talk, or tried to, at least.

After that night, I began to drop by Bantan more and more frequently; only when there were no customers, of course. Talking with Ayako-san (the owner) really helped improve my Japanese, and I eventually started coming when there were other customers. She introduced me to all of them and we all became good friends. But my relationship with Ayako-san was particularly special. She eventually went so far as to refer to herself as my "Japanese mother," and since she had no children of her own, I felt this was a compliment of the highest degree.

Over the next four or so years, I would go to Bantan three or four nights a week. I met a lot of amazing people and developed great relationships there. I'm sure if you look hard enough, you'll be able to find your own little Bantan too. If you ever do somehow make it out to Nagasaki, be sure to stop by and you can ask Ayako-san about me (also, I recommend trying the champon. It's amazing!).

Chapter 17: Useful Links

Throughout this book, I have talked about a few online organizations and listed a couple websites I found useful during my attempts to land a teaching job abroad. Here, you'll find all of those (and a few extra ones not mentioned above) in one place for your convenience.

www.aeonet.com – If you're looking to teach in Japan, AEON is definitely the route I would go (especially for those with no teaching experience). I worked there for over four years, and had an absolutely wonderful experience. If you end up working in Kyuushuu, you can tell them at their headquarters that Jeremy sent you (It's been a few years since I left, but I'm sure they'll still remember me). Another good thing about AEON is that they accept applications year-round, which can help make life a little easier for your if you're looking to go to Japan.

www.ajarn.com – If Thailand is where you think you'd like to head off to, then Ajarn is most likely your best bet for finding job placement.

www.CIEE.org/teach – Through CIEE, you can find jobs in a variety of countries; Chile, China, the Czech

Republic, Dominican Republic, Morocco, Peru, Senegal, South Korea, Spain, Thailand, and Vietnam.

I found a volunteer position in Spain through CIEE and had an absolutely AMAZING experience. The only problem people may have is that *you* have to actually pay *them* money to get you a position abroad. Most of the time, the position you receive will be a paid one. So, you should make back the money you pay them to get you out there in the first place. I understand that that may be a problem for some people, but I can tell you, from my experience anyway, that they are a well-organized and trustworthy organization. And no, they are not paying me to say this (though, I wouldn't be opposed to getting a little kick-back from any potential income this book's readers may generate, in case any CIEE employee happens to be reading...).

www.daveseslcafe.com – Here you can find hundreds of job listings for English teaching positions all over the world. You'll also find useful and interesting articles, links, and even a message board where you can communicate with others much like yourself.

www.greataupair.com – If teaching at a school isn't your thing, or you're looking for something more in the short-term, being an au pair might be perfect for you. At this site you can create a profile (information about you, your experience, etc.) and put it out there for families to see.

You can choose whether or not to pay money for a subscription. Theoretically, it is completely free. Paying money, however, gives you the ability to message families you're interested in, instead of only being able to have *them* message *you* (which obviously increases your chances of finding a family).

www.internationalteflacademy.com – This is a fantastic resource for all things related to teaching abroad. In addition to offering TEFL courses and job placement, you can also find a plethora of articles related to teaching and living abroad. Whether or not you want to find work through the International TEFL Academy, you should definitely take advantage of the free information they provide.

www.jetprogramusa.org – If you feel like Japan is where you want to teach, then the Jet Program could be a good option for you. With Jet, you'll be working at a public school, and will most likely have a little "easier" of a job than you would have otherwise working at a training center. Just remember that time-wise getting a position with Jet can be a little difficult. So, be sure to get all of your paper work and other required documents/materials in as soon as you can. If you miss the deadline, you'll have to wait a *whole* year before they begin accepting applications again.

www.liveworkplayjapan.com – If you're planning on going to Japan to find work, this is a great source. My pal Martin is part owner of this website, and has a lot of great information to offer about living, working, and playing in Japan (perhaps that's where the name comes from...). The site's mission is to "inform people about the boundless opportunities for success and enriching life experience in Japan." We recently did a podcast together which you should be able to find on his site.

www.lonleyplanet.com – Odds are, if you're interested at all in traveling, you have heard of Lonely Planet. If not, then this is an amazing site to learn just about everything you would want to know about your target destination. It doesn't offer much information in the way of teaching English or working abroad, but it can give you a lot of great information about the sights and other details regarding accommodations, the local transportation system, medical care, and the like.

www.nihongoshark.com – This is another website owned and operated by another pal of mine by the name of Niko. He offers a couple of different courses for learning Japanese (one of them being *completely* free) and regularly offers different articles that teach the language. A great source for anyone serious about learning Japanese. You may even find a couple of articles written by yours truly on his site, from time to time.

www.numbeo.com – Numbeo offers a plethora of information on cities around the world, from statistics on crime to health care. Their cost-of-living database is also really impressive, and you should definitely search your target destination to find out how much money you can expect to spend and save while abroad.

www.ontesol.com – There are hundreds of companies and organizations through which you can get a TESOL/TEFL certification (I haven't actually counted them, but I am confident that there are at least hundreds), and I don't have any experience with other organizations upon which to base a preference for this particular organization, but this was the website I personally used to get my 100+ hour TESOL certification. I did all of my coursework online and didn't have any problems. The certification I got from Ontesol was essential in getting my current job here in China. You can certainly go through any school or company you want, but I thought that by listing one I used and know can be trusted would help cut-down a lot of research time on your part.

www.searchassociates.com – I have never personally used Search Associates, but it is one of the most highly regarded companies for connecting teachers with international schools. They do not specifically find a position at a school for you, but instead help you connect with potential employers via their database or even actual job fairs you can attend in person. You create a profile and are informed when a school that fits your preferences posts an opening. The service they provide will cost $225 for a three year period (a bargain, if you ask me). You are not guaranteed to find a position, but they boast a 70% success rate.

www.teachaway.com – This is a *free* service that will help you find work abroad in a number of countries (13 as of the time of this writing). You can register online and start sifting through potential positions. Most jobs offered here require at the very least a Bachelor's degree. Though, their volunteer programs have no such requirements. So, there should be something here for everyone.

www.TEFL.net – This is a website that offers a plethora of information for current and would-be ESL teachers alike.

www.transitionsabroad.com – Transitions Abroad doesn't only focus on helping individuals find teaching positions abroad, they offer a wide variety of avenues to go down; such as volunteer opportunities, summer jobs, internships, au pair placement, and even farm jobs abroad! If being a teacher isn't exactly what you're into (and you'd perhaps rather throw bales of hay), you can certainly find something here that would better suit your preferences.

Thank you

That is going to do it for any information or advice I can dispense to you, dear reader. Thank you very much for taking the time to read my book. Even though it is fairly short, I spent quite a bit of time working on it. I truly hope that you found it useful and worth your time.

I'd also like to thank my friends and family for putting up with my "constant" trekking of the globe. I don't know when, but I really do plan on eventually settling down in one place some day. Though, I don't necessarily know if it will be in the U.S... (sorry Mom!)

Anyway, my friend, I wish you luck in your efforts to make it abroad and in all of your adventures hence. If you can have even a *fraction* of the amazing experiences I have had, then all of the time and hard work you put into finding a job will definitely be worth it. Happy teaching and adventuring!

Jeremy "Some Guy" Rasmussen

Me conquering Mt. Fuji on one of my own adventures

Check out my homepage at:
www.LearnJapaneseFromSomeGuy.com

My Japanese grammar textbook:
www.amazon.com/dp/B013D2FDMG

My YouTube channel:
youtube.com/c/learnjapanesefromsomeguy